Post your finished work and join the community.

#FAITHINCOLOR

IN HIS PRESENCE

ADULT COLORING BOOK With JOURNAL

PASSIO

These words, how they should cheer thee,

When troubled and distress'd,

My presence shall go with thee,

And I will give thee rest.

—LIZZIE ASHBACH
"My Presence Shall Go With Thee"

Surrounded by Your Glory

Having faith in God is more than just believing in His existence. It is knowing that you are always walking in His presence. He is your Father, your Healer, your Redeemer, and your everlasting joy. He wants to guide and direct you. Seek Him, and He will reveal His desires for you.

The Bible says that when you draw near to God, He will draw near to you. So as you color, enter His presence. Journal your prayers and record what your heavenly Father reveals to you. You can also praise Him for His faithfulness, which will build your faith and help you believe that He is able to meet every need that you face now or in your future. You can trust Him and continue to praise Him. And when you do, His peace, "which surpasses all understanding, will protect your hearts and minds through Christ Jesus" (Phil. 4:7).

We've placed these carefully selected verses from Scripture on the facing page of each design. Each one was chosen to complement the illustration while inspiring you to enter His presence. As you color these designs, reflect quietly on God's goodness and the many gifts He has bestowed upon you. When you are encouraged by God's promises to love and care for you, you will find that the cares and worries of life melt away.

It might interest you to know that the verses in this book are taken from the Modern English Version of the Holy Bible. The Modern English Version (MEV) is the most modern translation produced in the King James tradition within the last thirty years. This formal equivalence translation maintains the beauty of the past yet provides fresh clarity for a new generation of Bible readers. If you would like more information on the MEV, please visit www.mevbible.com.

We hope you find this coloring book to be both beautiful and inspirational. As you color, remember that the best artistic endeavors have no rules. Unleash your creativity as you experiment with colors, textures, and mediums. Freedom of self-expression will help to release wellness, balance, mindfulness, and inner peace into your life, allowing you to enjoy the process as well as the finished product. When you're finished, you can frame your favorite creations for displaying or gift giving. Then post your artwork on Facebook, Twitter, or Instagram with the hashtag #FAITHINCOLOR.

In Your presence is fullness of joy.

—PSALM 16:11B, MEV

_____

_____

_____

_____

_____

_____

_____

_____

_____

_____

_____

_____

_____

_____

_____

_____

In
Your presence
is FULLNESS
of joy

— Psalm 16:11

My Presence will go with you, and I will give you rest.

—*EXODUS 33:14*, MEV

_____

_____

_____

_____

_____

_____

_____

_____

_____

_____

_____

_____

_____

_____

_____

_____

_____

Let us come before His presence with thanksgiving;

let us make a joyful noise unto Him with psalms!

—Psalm 95:2, MEV

_____

_____

_____

_____

_____

_____

_____

_____

_____

_____

_____

_____

_____

_____

_____

_____

_____

Serve the LORD with gladness;

come before His presence with singing.

—PSALM 100:2, MEV

Likewise, I tell you, there is joy in the presence of

the angles of God over one sinner who repents.

—LUKE 15:10, MEV

_____
_____
_____
_____
_____
_____
_____
_____
_____
_____
_____
_____
_____
_____
_____
_____
_____

For You place blessings on him forever;

You make him rejoice with gladness with Your presence.

—Psalm 21:6, MEV

_____

_____

_____

_____

_____

_____

_____

_____

_____

_____

_____

_____

_____

_____

_____

_____

There is therefore now no condemnation for those who are in Christ Jesus, who walk not according to the flesh, but according to the Spirit. For the law of the Spirit of life in Christ Jesus has set me free from the law of sin and death.

—ROMANS 8:1–2, MEV

Peace I leave with you. My peace I give to you. Not as the world gives do I give to you. Let not your heart be troubled, neither let it be afraid.

—John 14:27, mev

Remember, I am with you,

and I will protect you wherever you go.

—GENESIS 28:15A, MEV

_____

_____

_____

_____

_____

_____

_____

_____

_____

_____

_____

_____

_____

_____

_____

The tabernacle of God is with men, and He will dwell with them. They shall be His people, and God Himself will be with them and be their God.

—*Revelation 21:3b, MEV*

_____

_____

_____

_____

_____

_____

_____

_____

_____

_____

_____

_____

_____

_____

_____

_____

Even though I walk through the valley of the shadow of death,

I will fear no evil; for You are with me;

Your rod and Your staff, they comfort me.

—PSALM 23:4, MEV

Surely goodness and mercy shall follow me all the days of my

life, and I will dwell in the house of the LORD forever.

—PSALM 23:6, MEV

_____

_____

_____

_____

_____

_____

_____

_____

_____

_____

_____

_____

_____

_____

_____

_____

And remember, I am with you always, even to the end of the age.

—MATTHEW 28:20B, MEV

_____
_____
_____
_____
_____
_____
_____
_____
_____
_____
_____
_____
_____
_____
_____
_____
_____
_____

If...you will seek the LORD your God, you will find Him, if you seek Him with all your heart and with all your soul.

—DEUTERONOMY 4:29, MEV

_____
_____
_____
_____
_____
_____
_____
_____
_____
_____
_____
_____
_____
_____
_____
_____
_____
_____

For the LORD your God has blessed you

in all the works of your hands.

—DEUTERONOMY 2:7, MEV

*You shall love the L*ORD *your God with all your heart*

and with all your soul and with all your might.

—D*EUTERONOMY* 6:5, MEV

If you listen to these judgments, keep them, and do them,

then the LORD your God shall keep with you the covenant and

the mercy which He swore to your fathers.

—DEUTERONOMY 7:12, MEV

_____

_____

_____

_____

_____

_____

_____

_____

_____

_____

_____

_____

_____

_____

_____

_____

The LORD your God is He that goes with you,

to fight for you against your enemies, to save you.

—DEUTERONOMY 20:4, MEV

_____

_____

_____

_____

_____

_____

_____

_____

_____

_____

_____

_____

_____

_____

_____

_____

_____

_____

Do not be afraid or dismayed, for the L<small>ORD</small> your God

is with you wherever you go.

—J<small>OSHUA</small> 1:9<small>C</small>, <small>MEV</small>

*The L*ORD* our God be with us, as He was with our fathers.*

Let Him neither leave us nor forsake us.

*—1 K*INGS* 8:57,* MEV

Do all that is in your heart, for God is with you.

—1 CHRONICLES 17:2, MEV

_____
_____
_____
_____
_____
_____
_____
_____
_____
_____
_____
_____
_____
_____
_____
_____
_____

Be strong and courageous, and take action. Do not be afraid

nor be dismayed for the LORD God, my God, is with you. He will

not leave you nor forsake you, until you have finished all the

work of the service of the house of the LORD.

—1 CHRONICLES 28:20, MEV

_____
_____
_____
_____
_____
_____
_____
_____
_____
_____
_____
_____
_____
_____
_____
_____
_____

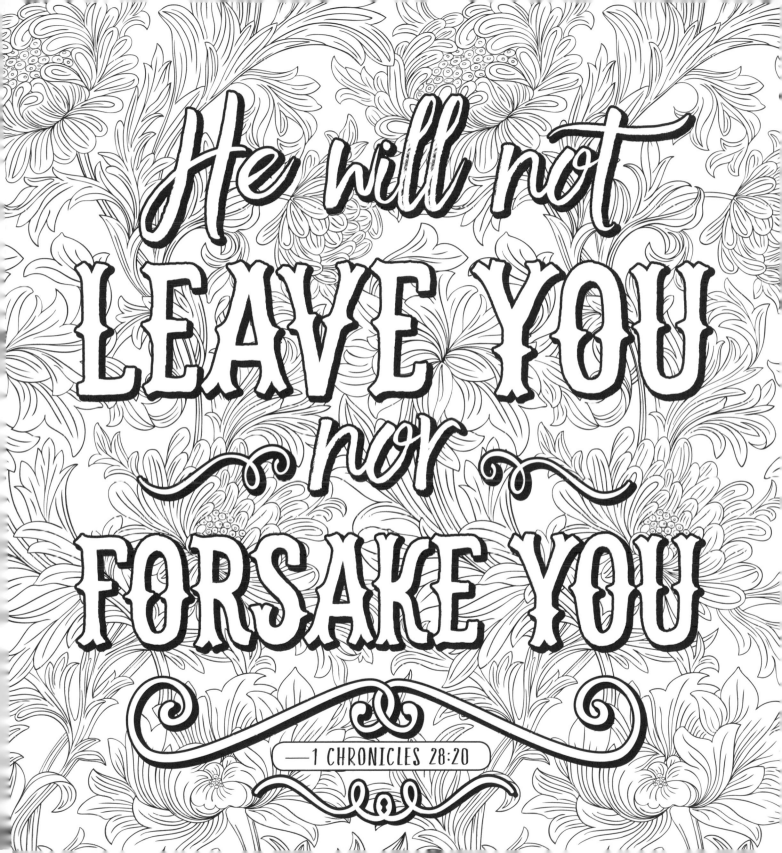

God is with the generation of the righteous.

—Psalm 14:5, MEV

Be strong and of a good courage. Fear not, nor be afraid of

them, for the LORD *your God, it is He who goes with you.*

He will not fail you, nor forsake you.

—DEUTERONOMY *31:6,* MEV

_____

_____

_____

_____

_____

_____

_____

_____

_____

_____

_____

_____

_____

_____

_____

_____

_____

Hope in God, for I will yet thank Him

for the help of His presence.

—PSALM 42:5C, MEV

Yet the LORD will command His lovingkindness in the daytime, and in the night His song will be with me, a prayer to the God of my life.

—PSALM 42:8, MEV

_____

_____

_____

_____

_____

_____

_____

_____

_____

_____

_____

_____

_____

_____

_____

_____

_____

_____

God is my helper; the Lord is with those who support my life.

—PSALM 54:4, MEV

Do not fear, for I am with you; do not be dismayed, for I am your God. I will strengthen you, I will help you, yes, I will uphold you with My righteous right hand.

—Isaiah 41:10, MEV

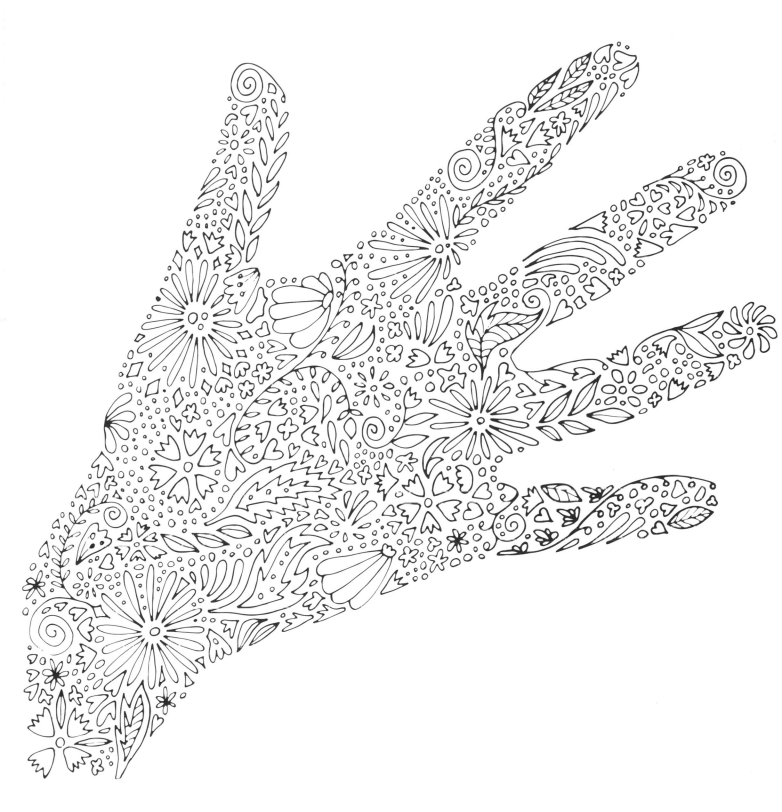

*For the L*ORD *will go before you,*

and the God of Israel will be your rear guard.

—I*SAIAH* 52:12*B, MEV*

*I will give them a heart to know Me, that I am the L*ORD*; and they will be My people, and I will be their God, for they will return to Me with their whole heart.*

*—J*EREMIAH *24:7,* MEV

Thus shall they know that I, the LORD their God, am with them, and that they, the house of Israel, are My people, says the Lord GOD.

—EZEKIEL 34:30, MEV

_____

_____

_____

_____

_____

_____

_____

_____

_____

_____

_____

_____

_____

_____

_____

_____

I, the LORD their God, am with them

—EZEKIEL 34:30

You shall love the Lord your God with all your heart,

and with all your soul, and with all your mind.

—*Matthew 22:37,* MEV

For with God all things are possible.

—MARK 10:27B, MEV

_____

_____

_____

_____

_____

_____

_____

_____

_____

_____

_____

_____

_____

_____

_____

_____

_____

When he arrived and saw the grace of God, he rejoiced and

exhorted them all to remain with the Lord with a loyal heart.

—ACTS 11:23, MEV

_____

_____

_____

_____

_____

_____

_____

_____

_____

_____

_____

_____

_____

_____

_____

_____

Brothers, let every man, in whatever condition

he is called, remain there with God.

—1 C*ORINTHIANS* 7:24, *MEV*

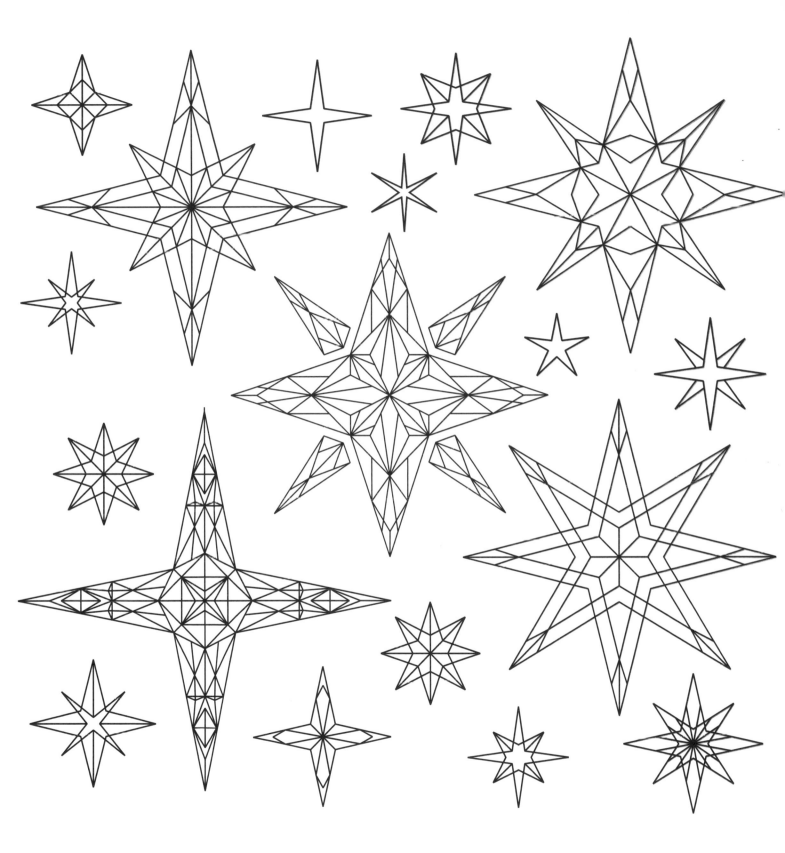

God is faithful, and He will not permit you to be tempted above what you can endure, but will with the temptation also make a way to escape.

—1 CORINTHIANS 10:13B, MEV

_____
_____
_____
_____
_____
_____
_____
_____
_____
_____
_____
_____
_____
_____
_____
_____
_____
_____

But God, being rich in mercy, because of His great love

with which He loved us, even when we were dead in sins,

made us alive together with Christ.

—Ephesians 2:4–5, MEV

Do those things which you have both learned and received, and heard and seen in me, and the God of peace will be with you.

—PHILIPPIANS 4:9, MEV

Do not forget to do good and to share.

For with such sacrifices God is well pleased.

—Hebrews 13:16, MEV

_____

_____

_____

_____

_____

_____

_____

_____

_____

_____

_____

_____

_____

_____

_____

If any of you lacks wisdom, let him ask of God, who gives to all

men liberally and without criticism, and it will be given to him.

—JAMES 1:5, MEV

Grace, mercy, and peace will be with you from God the Father and

from the Lord Jesus Christ, the Son of the Father, in truth and love.

—2 JOHN 3, MEV

Righteousness and justice are the foundation of Your throne;

mercy and truth shall go before Your presence.

—PSALM 89:14, MEV

_____
_____
_____
_____
_____
_____
_____
_____
_____
_____
_____
_____
_____
_____
_____
_____

Seek the LORD and His strength; seek His presence continuously.

—*PSALM 105:4, MEV*

Seek the LORD and His STRENGTH

—PSALM 105:4

And now, O Father, glorify Me in Your own presence with the glory which I had with You before the world existed.

—JOHN 17:5, MEV

And His name, by faith in His name, has made this man strong, whom you see and know. And faith which comes through Him has given him perfect health in your presence.

—ACTS 3:16, MEV

Seek good and not evil, so that you may live; then the Lord, the

God of Hosts, will truly be with you, as you claim.

—*Amos 5:14, MEV*

_____

_____

_____

_____

_____

_____

_____

_____

_____

_____

_____

_____

_____

_____

_____

Seek GOOD and not EVIL, so that you may LIVE

—AMOS 5:14

Most Charisma House Book Group products are available at special quantity discounts for bulk purchase for sales promotions, premiums, fund-raising, and educational needs. For details, write Charisma House Book Group, 600 Rinehart Road, Lake Mary, Florida 32746, or telephone (407) 333-0600.

In His Presence Adult Coloring Book With Prayer Journal published by Passio
Charisma Media/Charisma House Book Group
600 Rinehart Road
Lake Mary, Florida 32746
www.charismahouse.com

Design Director: Justin Evans
Cover Design: Justin Evans
Interior Design: Justin Evans, Lisa Rae McClure, Vincent Pirozzi

Illustrations: Getty Images/Depositphotos

International Standard Book Number: 978-1-62998-963-1

First edition

16 17 18 19 20 — 987654321

Printed in the United States of America